History Through Poetry
World War I

Paul Dowswell

WAYLAND

an imprint of Hodder Children's Books

raid

~-1956

...me old view,
...oming tame,
...othing new,
...ery same,
...r front,
...ll four,
...d 'unt,
...r.

'Blighters'

Siegfried Sassoon (1886–1...

The House is crammed: tier ...
And cackle at the Show,
Of harlots shrill the c...
'We're sure the Kaise...

I'd like to see ...
Lurching to ...

And th...
To m...

Happy is England Now

John Freeman (1880–1929)

Happy is England in the brave that die
For wrongs not hers and wrongs so sternly hers;
Happy in those that give, give, and endure
The pain that never the new years may cure;
Happy in all her dark woods, green fields, towns,
Her hills and rivers and her chafing sea.

…happiest is England now
In those that fight, and watch with pride and
tears.

(1914)

sternly
In the context of the poem, the word means unquestionably, or without a doubt.

endure
To suffer something without giving up.

chafing
Rubbing against. The poet is referring to the sea which completely surrounds the border of Britain.

This is an extract from a patriotic poem written in 1914 at the outbreak of World War I. Here, the verse begins by boldly declaring that Britain is glad to send its soldiers to die in battle, because they are fighting a just cause. It also suggests, in the phrase, 'wrongs so sternly hers', that Britain too bears responsibility for the circumstances that have led to war. The poem acknowledges that the war will bring grief, but its description of the English landscape is intended to evoke pride in the reader, and suggest that the sacrifice to come will be worthwhile.

World War I, also known as the Great War, lasted from 1914 to 1918. It was the first 'modern' war. There were tanks, aeroplanes, machine-guns and submarines – almost all the technology which we think of today as being the tools of modern warfare. But the societies that fought the war were very different from our own.

Europe at the start of the twentieth century was not the closely-knit community it is today. Instead there were bitter rivalries. The continent was divided into two camps, each committed to defending their allies. In one camp were Germany, Austria-Hungary and Italy. In the other were France, Russia and Britain. World War I began because Austria-Hungary and Russia went to war over territory in Eastern Europe, and the other partners in the rival power blocs were dragged into the conflict as a result.

There were other reasons too. Many European countries had colonies – territories in other continents which they controlled and exploited. Although Germany was a very powerful nation, she had few colonies, and was building a large navy to help her gain more territory. Britain, then the richest and most powerful nation on earth, felt threatened by Germany's growing strength.

Many nations, including Britain, feared Germany's growing power. This cartoon shows the German leader, the Kaiser, as 'The Glutton' (greedy eater), trying to consume the world.

The event that 'sparked' World War I was the assassination of the leader of Austria-Hungary, Archduke Franz Ferdinand. The assassin, Gavrilo Princip, was quickly arrested, as shown here, and later died in prison.

POET'S CORNER

John Freeman was a businessman and civil servant by profession, as well as an established poet. Many poems were written in Britain at the outbreak of World War I, but his are the most patriotic and emotional.

Les Soliloques du Soldat (The Soldier's Soliloquies, I)

Marc De Larreguy De Civrieux (1895–1916)

After the Charleroi affair
And since we waved the Marne goodbye,
I drag my carcass everywhere,
But never know the reason why.

In trench and barn I spend each day,
From fort or attic glimpse the sky,
At this war simply slog away,
But never know the reason why.

I ask, hoping to understand
This slaughter's purpose. The reply
I get is: 'For the Motherland!'
But never know the reason why.

(1916)

As the fighting dragged on, troops on all sides grew increasingly weary. In this extract the poet mentions two battles at the start of the war where French soldiers fought bravely to stop the German army overrunning their country. Now, two years later in 1916, the war has reached a stalemate and the exhausted writer wonders why they are still fighting. The trite patriotism of 'For the Motherland!' no longer inspires his weary body.

The French lost more soldiers on the Western Front than any other nation. In the first two weeks of the war 300,000 men were killed or wounded. Dreadful slaughter at battles like Verdun saw French casualties rise to over 5.5 million by the end of the war (1,385,300 of these were killed).

Looking back, many people wonder why soldiers allowed themselves to be led to their deaths in such huge numbers. At the time, most soldiers were obedient to their officers in a way that would be unthinkable in today's less reverential societies. Military discipline at the Front was also very harsh. Cowardice or desertion was punished by firing squad. During attacks, military policemen patrolled the trenches, ready to shoot dead any soldier who did not go over the top when the signal was given.

POET'S CORNER

Marc De Larreguy De Civrieux was barely 21 when he was killed at Verdun in 1916. He wrote several poems about the unthinking patriotism that made the French government carry on fighting.

Troops prepare for an attack. Their courage is boosted by the grim fact that they will be shot by their own officers if they fail to 'go over the top'.

A cartoon depicting the French mutiny in 1917. An officer attempts to inspire his troops, with little success.

Occasionally there were rebellions. In June 1917 half the French army mutinied – the military term for refusing to obey orders. The French authorities acted swiftly. The mutiny was kept secret, and reforms such as more home leave and better rations were introduced. In Russia, mutinous troops cost their country the war. When soldiers refused to carry on fighting the Russians surrendered huge chunks of territory to Germany, and a communist regime seized power.

Glossary

Difficult words from the verse appear alongside each poem. This glossary explains words used in the main text. The page numbers are given so that you can study the glossary and then see how the words have been used.

ardent (p. 6) Eager, often unthinkingly or unquestioningly so.

biased (p. 18) Presenting only one side of an argument or view of events.

communism (p. 13) A political belief in which the state controls the wealth and industry of a country on behalf of the people.

evoke (p. 4) To conjure up a feeling or image.

exploit (p. 5) Make use of, often unfairly.

'go over the top' (p. 17) A phrase used by troops during the war to mean to charge against the enemy. To do this they had to 'go over the top' of their trenches and into no man's land.

hue and cry (p. 26) A loud noise made by a crowd.

infantrymen (pp. 9, 21) Soldiers belonging to a regiment of foot-soldiers.

innovative (p. 8) Daringly new and experimental.

Military Cross (p. 27) A medal awarded to British soldiers for outstanding bravery.

mutiny (p. 17) A revolt in the armed services, usually when men refuse to obey orders.

naïve (p. 20) Over-trusting; a tendency to believe something without questioning it.

no man's land (pp. 10, 21) The space between two opposing armies. On the Western Front this was the shell-torn landscape between the Allied and German trenches.

patriotic (p. 4) Having a deep love and loyalty for one's country.

perceptions (p. 23) Opinions and ideas.

power blocs (p. 5) Groups of countries that have joined together to defend their mutual interests against a common enemy.

pride (p. 4) A sense of one's own worth compared to others.

propaganda (pp. 12, 18) Biased news and information put out by a government to convince its citizens that a particular viewpoint or policy is right.

reconnaissance (p. 23) A survey of enemy positions and strength.

repellent (p. 19) Deeply unpleasant or disgusting.

romantic (pp. 6, 7, 22) Unrealistically glamorous.

sacrifice (p. 4) To give up something precious, especially one's own life, for a worthwhile cause.

sentiment (p. 6) A deeply felt idea.

strategy (p. 12) The art of moving troops, ships, aircraft etc. into favourable positions.

tarry (p. 11) To remain, linger.

trenches (pp. 8, 10, 11, 17, 19) Lines of ditches, fortified by sandbags and barbed wire, which soldiers dug to protect themselves and defend their positions.

trite (p. 16) Stale or meaningless, as a result of overuse.

veterans (p. 29) Soldiers who have fought in a particular war.

Western Front (p. 8) The main battleground in western Europe, stretching from the Belgian coast to Switzerland.

BOOKS TO READ

For younger readers

A Children's English History in Verse
by Kenneth Baker (ed.)
(Faber, 1999)

Armistice 1918
by Reg Grant
(Hodder Wayland, 2000)

Faber Book of War Poetry
by Kenneth Baker (ed.)
(Faber, 1996)

General Haig: Butcher or War Winner?
by Josh Brooman
(Longman, 1998)

In Flanders Field: The Story of the Poem
by Linda Granfield
(Stoddart, 2000)

Some Corner of a Foreign Field
by James Bentley (ed.)
(Little, Brown and Co., 1992)

The War in the Trenches
by Ole Steen Hansen
(Hodder Wayland, 2000)

For older readers

Death's Men
by Dennis Winter
(Penguin Books, 1978)

The First World War
by A.J.P. Taylor
(Penguin Books, 1966)

The Great War and Modern Memory
by Paul Fussell
(Oxford University Press, 2000)

The Lost Voices of World War One
by Tim Cross
(Bloomsbury, 1988)

Up the Line to Death
by Brian Gardner (ed.)
(Methuen, 1964)

INDEX